"IM JUST SAYIN"

ELDER ZIMMERI C MCNEAL JR

JUST SAYIN'

DEDICATION

This book is dedicated to my grandfather, The late Apostle E. L. Kingcannon. A man of great honor who always taught me to never hold back and to never water down God's word. To always be honest and to tell it like it is despite what kind of response you may get.

ACKNOWLEDGMENTS

First of all, I would like to give honor God, my father in heaven. Without him none of this would be possible. I would like to thank my wife, Kimyetta McNeal for all her love and support. You're AWESOME BABY! Thanks to my mom and dad, Betty and Deryle Polk. You guys are the best, my biggest supporters, and my biggest fans. Thanks to my three children: Cherica, Aaron and Marquis. You all have kept me encouraged and inspired a lot of my writings. I would like to thank my entire family, especially Dear, Uncle David and Vinnie for all the love and support. My friends are too many to name, but you all know who you are. I love you guys especially those that stood by my side in the lowest point of my life: Cook, Aimee, Kevy Kev and Levantz just to name a few. Finally, I would like to thank my friend Tony Grebmeier. Listening to your story and the release of your journal brought me to this point. Now I have a book... LOL. I hope everyone enjoys the read and that it ministers to someone. None the less, just embrace it and remember that it's my opinion so don't be passing judgment. IM JUST SAYIN... LOL

PREFACE

Please read my words with an open mind and an open heart. These are my words, my beliefs and my outlook on life. Everyone is entitled to their own. The objective of this book is merely to inspire those who chose to read it and if you so choose to follow my belief structure after that then that's awesome. If you don't, that's cool, too. What I believe and what you believe may differ in some ways but one thing I can promise you is that if you do read this book, you will receive a blessing thru its words

IS IT LOVE

How strong is love?

Can love truly stand the test of time?

Can love heal all the hurt and pain inside?

I know that God's word says that love hopeth all things, and endureth all things and that love never fails. So, I guess what he is really trying to say is that it isn't love that's the problem... it's US!!!!!!
Loving oneself is often harder than loving others. Figure out how to love yourself before trying to love someone else. Our relationships are often tainted by the high standards that we set for ourselves. But the same thing happens when we set our standards too low as well. We often fall in love with how a person looks, how much money one has, what kind of car a person drives, what kind of house they live in. I could go on and on but what happens, the true test is when all that is gone and it's just you and that person, 50 said it best when he spit these lyrics:

- ✓ *It's easy to love me now*
- ✓ *Would you love me if I was down and out?*
- ✓ *If I fell off tomorrow would you still love me?*
- ✓ *If I didn't smell so good would you still hug me?*
- ✓ *If I got locked up and sentenced to a quarter century,*
  Could I count on you to be there to support me mentally?
- ✓ *If I went back to a hooptie from a Benz, would you poof and*
  disappear like some of my friends?
- ✓ *If I was hit and I was hurt would you be by my side?*
- ✓ *If it was time to put in work would you be down to ride?*

Love a person for who they are not what they have. Don't try to change them into who you want them to be, let them be who God wants them to be and then LOVE just might do what it was designed to do!

#IMJUSTSAYIN...

CAST YOUR BURDENS ON THE LORD

One cannot control what is not theirs to control, one cannot fix what is not theirs to fix, one cannot bend what is unbendable. One cannot carry what is not given to them to carry, one cannot bury what is not meant to be buried. One cannot heal if unwilling to be healed. One cannot shield if there is nothing to be shielded. One cannot force a square peg into a round hole...

#IMJUSTSAYIN...

Father I cast my cares on you because it's obvious that I'm not in control and I have really come to realize that this is how you want it so that you obtain the glory all by yourself so I move myself out of the way to allow you to be you in all areas of my life...

YOUR JOY IS BY YOUR OWN HAND

Today is a new day. Don't let the devil still your joy because he will if you let him. You're not alone even if you feel that you are. God loves you and the victory has already been won. Be positive minded in everything you do today and watch how smooth your day goes. Ignore anyone and anything that introduces conflict into your circle of life. It's just the enemy trying to steal the bountiful blessings God has planned for you today. Be a conqueror, and not a victim of your own circumstances. Be the driving force behind your own success.

#IMJUSTSAYIN...

THINGS CHANGE

Be content in everything that you do today. Sometimes your plans change, but that doesn't mean that the situation has changed. Just your plan has changed. Maybe it changed for the better, maybe it wasn't the right time. You should just make the best of the change and make the best of every situation today. Just remember to stay in the driver's seat and drive your success home...

#IMJUSTSAYIN...

THINKING ABOUT THE FUTURE

One day, maybe it will happen.
One day maybe you will see it.
One day maybe it will be.
One day maybe you will feel it.
One day maybe you will have it.
One day maybe you can reach out and grab it.
ONE DAY...
But, until then...
KEEP IT PUSHIN...

#IMJUSTSAYIN...

Romans 8:28, King James Version (KJV)
"And we know that all things work together for good of them that love God, to them who are called according to his purpose."

FEAR IS THE DEVIL

As you awaken from a blissful slumber, meditate on this word from God today...

"NEVER LET FEAR DECIDE YOUR FUTURE"

You can't always wait for the perfect moment. Sometimes you must let go and dare to do it, because life is too short to wonder what could have been. When time passes by it's too late and you will waste a whole lot of time worrying about what should have been. Your future awaits you along with the fulfillment of all your dreams. Don't let fear stand in the way, because if you do your dreams will remain dreams and never manifest into your future...

#IMJUSTSAYIN...

SUFFERING IS A PREREQUISITE TO SUCCESS

OK now let this little message marinate in your spirit today and you just might get the revelation of your current situation.

As you look back over your life, you see some of the things that you're currently going thru or maybe something that you just went thru, but not quite sure what is happening or what just happened. Don't over analyze the situation. Just realize that everything happens for a reason, the good and the bad. Some things are unexpected and some you can see coming from a mile away. All you can really do is roll with the punches. Something is going on that's preparing you for the next phase of your life, so don't fight it. Roll with it and see where God is taking you. He may be preparing you for your greatest comeback ever.

#IMJUSTSAYIN...

AND THIS TOO SHALL PASS

Your suffering is temporary.
Your pain is temporary.
Your misery is temporary.
Your brokenness is temporary.
Walk in what you want from God rather you see it or not.
The end to your suffering lies there.
The cure to your pain lies there.
The end to your misery lies there.
The repairs to your brokenness await you there.

#IMJUSTSAYIN...

2 Corinthians 4:17-18. "For our light affliction, which is but for a moment, worketh for us a far more exceeding and eternal weight of glory; While we look not at the things which are seen, but at the things which are not seen: for the things which are seen are temporal; but the things which are not seen are eternal."

TAKE THE TEST

All things aren't bad. Things happen for a reason and are just tests.

To test your strength.
To test your faith.
To test your bond.
To test your endurance.
To test your love.

Failing them is not guaranteed, unless you give up...

#IMJUSTSAYIN...

PRAY

James 5:16 "The effectual fervent prayer of a righteous man availeth much"

This sometimes seems unreal, hard to reach daily. Thoughts of, "am I truly righteous, does God really hear me, will he look at things I may have done and turn away from me." We all have these thoughts, making it hard to pray. But if we can manage to muster enough time and get rid of all the distractions, there is an amazing promise that God has given to us thru Prayer. Prayer offers life, strength and break through. It offers us closeness with God in which our comfort lies. It breaks the stress and monotony of our present issues caused by our past choices. It provides courses of action for our future. Prayer changes things especially if you believe. Take the time to break away from the many distractions of today and find some time to pray. It works. Trust me when I say it has been a long time coming. Maybe you should try it.

#IMJUSTSAYIN...

FOCUS IS KEY

YO!! Guard your heart today, let nothing come in between you and your inner peace. God's work is beginning, and your success and destiny are being revealed. Things will happen today that will try to destroy your vision and focus. Be aware, keep a constant prayer inside and avoid altercation. Hey, it's going to be a beautiful day. Let's go get it...

#IMJUSTSAYIN...

Phillipians 4:7-9
7 "And the peace of God, which passes all understanding, shall keep your hearts and minds through Christ Jesus."
8 "Finally, brethren, whatsoever things are true, whatsoever things are honest, whatsoever things are just, whatsoever things are pure, whatsoever things are lovely, whatsoever things are of good report; if there be any virtue, and if there be any praise, think on these things."
9 "Those things, which ye have both learned, and received, and heard, and seen in me, do: and the God of peace shall be with you."

BAD COUNSEL

Okay ya'll, this was deep for me... So, I'm going to hit you with this.

Be careful of the counsel you seek. What I'm learning is that some of them are your biggest haters, the things they tell you seem all well and good, but it has an underlying agenda. Have you ever noticed the positive nature of some people's advice always seem to try and trick you into being content with where you are and not following your dreams? "Well you got a good job be thankful cause some people don't have a job." You know something, regardless of how thankful we can and should be, it doesn't mean we can't shoot for the stars. Don't let people use positive influences to kill your dreams....

#IMJUSTSAYIN...

BewareFalsePROPHETS

Jeremiah 29: 9-14
9 "They are prophesying lies to you in my name. I have not sent them,"
declares the LORD."
10 "This is what the LORD says: "When seventy years are completed for
Babylon, I will come to you and fulfill my good promise to bring you back to
this place."
11 "For I know the plans I have for you," declares the LORD, "plans to
prosper you and not to harm you, plans to give you hope and a future."
12 "Then you will call on me and come and pray to me, and I will listen to
you."
13 "You will seek me and find me when you seek me with all your heart."
14 I will be found by you," declares the LORD, "and will bring you back from
captivity. I will gather you from all the nations and places where I have
banished you," declares the LORD, "and will bring you back to the place from
which I carried you into exile."

THE DESIRES OF YOUR HEART

Sometimes we can get so distracted by the things we want. Like Success, Money, Love, Companionship. We get so caught up in all that, that we tend to forget the things we need. And sometimes what we want isn't always what we need at that given moment, but we want what we want none the less. Our inner most desires end up over shadowing the path that can get us the things I mentioned earlier. Though our Father said that he will give us the desires of our heart we must understand the path and the process for him doing that. Disappointments will happen along the way because we didn't get something we wanted at the time we wanted it but know that in time if you stay on the path all things will be fulfilled. But, one must remember that it is all in his timing not ours. Because he knows what we need even before we need it.

#IMJUSTSAYIN...

Matthew 6:25-34
25 "Therefore I say to you, do not worry about your life, what you will eat or what you will drink; nor about your body, what you will put on. Is not life more than food and the body more than clothing? 26 Look at the birds of the air, for they neither sow nor reap nor gather into barns; yet your heavenly Father feeds them. Are you not of more value than they? 27 Which of you by worrying can add one cubit to his stature?"
28 "So why do you worry about clothing? Consider the lilies of the field, how they grow: they neither toil nor spin; 29 and yet I say to you that even Solomon in all his glory was not arrayed like one of these. 30 Now if God so clothes the grass of the field, which today is, and tomorrow is thrown into the oven, will He not much more clothe you, O you of little faith?"
31 "Therefore do not worry, saying, 'What shall we eat?' or 'What shall we drink?' or 'What shall we wear?' 32 For after all these things the Gentiles seek. For your heavenly Father knows that you need all these things. 33 But seek first the kingdom of God and His righteousness, and all these things shall be added to you. 34 Therefore do not worry about tomorrow, for tomorrow will worry about its own things. Sufficient for the day is its own trouble."

REPENTANCE

It's amazing the things that people get offended over. That's why we have repentance, because you never know what you've done, what you said or what you've posted that will offend someone. Some things you know you said or done were offensive, others catch you off guard. Mostly because the person you offended is the only one that knows they were offended. So, I say repent daily for all things. Because the last thing you need is an altercation with someone because you said or did something that they didn't like that you had no clue about...

#IMJUSTSAYIN...

WHAT ARE YOU LOOKING FOR?

Sometimes we do things to prove a point just to realize that people are going to do whatever they want despite you, and despite your feelings. You slowly realize that maybe you don't even matter. But you do have worth in someone's eyes. This crazy world we live in, the crave for love, the crave for acceptance, the crave for attention, the crave to feel the slightest bit special to somebody, the crave for success, the crave for that one special someone to feel for you the way you feel for them. As well as the crave for respect.

These days it seems like the only thing we care about is what social media has to say but it's all a farce. All falsehood. If we focused as much attention on our walk with Christ, or whatever supreme being you serve, this world would be a better place. So sometimes those crazy things we do end up being failed attempts to prove whatever point we were trying to make, and you will still never be understood. And to prove that statement, think about something you did, said or posted that was totally out of character. People were probably like what in the heck is he/she up to? What is he/she doing? He/she know better than that. That's a shame... You can just hear all the negativity without it even being said. You can feel it pulling on your spirit. LOL. Everything has been taken totally out of context.

God has a mysterious way of teaching and showing us things. It's a message to the world to know your worth, a message that there's more to life than what Social Media and people have to say regarding what we do. We treat people's opinion like it's our GOD especially on social media. And we worship it, looking for what? I say this unto you all. Seek ye first the kingdom. Ten times out of ten what you're seeking is right in front of your face. You just can't see it, because you aren't looking.

#IMJUSTSAYIN...

FRET NOT

Things are a changing, GOD is rearranging. You are embarking on the area of your life where God is elevating you. So, now you got to stop complaining and worrying about all the people's mouth your name might be in. You have got to start restraining all the crazy thoughts in your brain and, suppress all the emotions from all the haters around you. Keep doing what you do. People are going to always find fault in you especially when you start to succeed. Jealousy will set in like wildfire and every chance a person gets they will try to tear you down, try to destroy your confidence in what you do. Let this lyric I wrote marinate in your spirit. It's based on my own experiences.

"I am drowning in my music. It keeps me from going insane. I really don't care who don't like it because it eases that inner pain. When, people come and go like the wind blows through the plains, you wonder why they live a lie, it's for the fortune and the fame. They forget the ones who had their back just to get to the next best thing, Man...

People come and go, they use you and abuse you. They want your knowledge and wisdom and disappear when you are empty. Then when success comes back your way and they can't partake. Then all of a sudden you ain't Shhhhh.... Well you know what I'm getting at.

#IMJUSTSAYIN...

PRAYER BREAK #1

Father thank you for another beautiful day to prove myself to you. Yesterday the evil one tried to ruin my evening, but I beat him. Give me the strength today to endure all the snares and traps he has setup for me this day. Bless everyone in my path both physical and virtual, in the mighty name of Jesus I pray. Amen.

The path for you has already been laid, stay on it. Those that are meant to be on it with you will be and those that aren't will fall by the way side.

#IMJUSTSAYIN...

JUDGE NOT

John 8:7 "When they continued to question Him, He straightened up and said to them, "Let him who is without sin among you be the first to cast a stone at her."

Stop judging people, especially on things that you know nothing about. Stop listening to people tell a story from thousands of miles away that were never present for the situation. Stop listening to people who gathered their intel from sources unknown. They are such great actors and story tellers that they tell these stories with compelling passion as if they were right there. Funny how that works... Judge not lest ye be judged yourself.

People get a kick out of exposing others. However, remember this: ALL DARKNESS WILL COME INTO THE LIGHT, no matter who you are and what status or title you hold, GOD is no respect of persons. So, as you pass judgement on others and are so quick to expose others, just remember that what goes around comes back around. What goes up must come down. YOU REAP WHAT YOU SOW!!!

#IMJUSTSAYIN...

IT'S GOING TO BE A GOOD DAY

Today is going to be a good day. Can you feel it? Satan is going to try to destroy what you may be building. He is going to try to destroy the path laid for your future. But peep this. You don't have to let it happen, because whatever you bind on earth is bound in heaven. "NO WEAPON FORMED AGAINST YOU SHALL PROSPER." Just understand that it is written that he is going to come and try to kill, steal, and destroy. It is also written that he is already defeated. So, if you know this already. Why continue to let it affect you? You already know the outcome and you also know what he's up to. Duhhh!!!

#IMJUSTSAYIN...

THERE IS MORE TO FEELING ALONE

There will always be times where you feel all alone. Times when you feel like no one understands you or that no one cares. Times where you feel alienated like a man with leprosy. I found that those times are the times we need to pay the most attention. Those are the times I believe God has put you in that special place that he wants you so that he can talk to you, in that place that has no distractions. We think of this the wrong way. Sometimes God is trying to reach us but we're wrapped up in so many things that we can't hear his voice, so he removes the distraction. When you feel that aloneness taking over your spirit, OPEN UP YOUR HEART AND SPIRITUAL EARS, AND LISTEN!!!

#IMJUSTSAYIN...

If you're feeling alone, and your weariness has grown, look up above, and thank God for His love. There's nothing you can do, to change His love for you; hold on friend, it's not the end. Something beautiful will come, the clouds will part for the sun, the skies will break for the Son, and the Father will say 'Well done.' But until then, until then, you're not alone. He can make bread from stone. Hold on to Him, and He'll hold on to you. Take one day at a time, pray for faith and be kind, and when forgetful becomes your mind, remember what He said, 'You are mine.'

~Nick Vujicic

REWARD IS IN THE SACRIFICE

Putting others needs before your own can be trying and exhausting. But, there is a reward in denying one's self to tend to others, to encourage others, to inspire others. There is a greater good being manifested in this practice. For it is written that it is better to give than it is to receive. Stay encouraged and keep up with this practice. It may be what you do best, and it just might be your purpose in life.

#IMJUSTSAYIN...

TWO FACED

I'm going to shed some light on some crazy stuff. With all the backbiting and talking about people behind peoples backs people tend to wonder why people don't want to be bothered. You try to be cordial and hospitable towards others just to find that they are smiling in your face all the while trying to take your place. Backstabbing, y 'all know the song. Well if you want to really understand why nobody wants to be bothered with you, just think about that for a moment. A lot of times it's the ones closest to us, and that person just might be you!!!

#IMJUSTSAYIN...

NOW FAITH IS

I saw a post on a family members Facebook page that really inspired me, and I wanted to share it with you in hopes to inspire you. I like what they wrote, but they didn't tell it right, so I'm going to break it down like this...

You can't say your faith is totally and completely in God if losing a relationship, a job, a car, a house, a dollar makes you lose your relationship with Him. Never let your love and trust in God be controlled by someone's love for you. Don't let your circumstances control your faith." NOW FAITH IS THE SUBSTANCE OF THINGS HOPED FOR AND THE EVIDENCE OF THINGS NOT SEEN... We get so caught up in our current situation that we can't even fathom the thought of believing in something that we cannot see, the thought of a better outcome. So, we lie in self-pity, tears, etc., like the world is over. Hope, what is it? It's something that we want to manifest in our lives. Our Faith is the substance of that. But can you see hope? Can you see what you are hoping for? Heck no, but Faith is also the evidence of that. What is Faith? From what I know it's your belief structure. You say you believe in God... But can you see him? No. You believe there is air and that we breathe it, can you see air? No. When you step out on faith you are walking in your belief in something that hasn't manifested yet, in other words you can't see it, or it hasn't happened yet, but you believe that it will... FAITH WITHOUT WORKS IS DEAD. You must do something to exercise your faith. Walking out your belief is works. Going thru the motions as if that thing is there, preparing things for what is yet to come... CALLING THOSE THINGS THAT BE NOT AS THOUGH THEY WERE... Losing things of this world should push us closer to God, not further away. Don't let the imperfections of others and the failures of life keep you away from a perfect God. He can change any situation, or move you into a better situation if you believe.

#IMJUSTSAYIN...

THE RESPONSE FROM GOD

When you have tried everything else, why not try me. I am the Lord thy God, supposedly the author and finisher of your faith. You done yet? Are you finished trying to do things your way? Are you done getting in my way? Ok, I will wait. I won't step in until you get done trying to fix things yourself. A word to the wise though, nothing is going to change until you let me handle it. You prayed and asked me to do it for you, but I can't because your stubborn behind is still trying to play my part. So, I'm just going to sit here and watch you suffer. Well it's what you want. I told you to leave the situation alone and let me deal with it, to let me handle it. I told you to cast your cares on my shoulders but nooooo, you just got to be disobedient. So, keep the pain and anguish that you nurse every day, it's what you want because if you didn't you would move and let me take control. So, crash and burn. And when you get tired, call me FOR REAL this time. And then, only then will I step in and help you. Until then, I got better things to do. Happy suffering.

#IMJUSTSAYIN...

Sincerely yours,

GOD...

THE PHARASEE SPIRIT

Have you ever felt like sometimes the things you do for others goes right thru them as if you have done nothing? As if what you do doesn't matter, making you feel like you don't even matter. You might feel like what you do is unappreciated and wonder what and why you even do it or keep subjecting yourself to that type of stress. A lot of what we do is for affection or something of that nature and when we don't receive it we feel like a failure and we find ourselves searching for something to fix, not realizing that maybe it isn't you. Maybe it's the hearts of others that's messed up. Maybe it's them that need to get it together. As for you, just because you're not openly acknowledged for the things you do does not mean your work has gone un-noticed, because if your heart is in the right place, God knows and God sees, and it is God who rewards. Trust, your treasures are being stored, and all of your good deeds are being tracked by him. And trust me when I say that they know it as well, and sometimes pride, position, reputation and image are some of the things that plagues the hearts of people, keeping them from seeing and or acknowledging it. All we can do is pray for them.

The Message is...
Don't do things for acknowledgement even though it makes you feel good and loved and all that, because when the outcome isn't what you were expecting, you beat yourself up. Don't do like the Pharisees did by doing things just to be seen. Do things out of love and compassion for others and their needs, filling a void in their lives. God is using you to answer prayers. Give out of your need, not only out of your abundance because your blessing lies in where your heart is when you give. It is so easy to help others when you have much but so much harder to do when your own lively hood is at stake. You will be rewarded whether it be on earth or in heaven. You're not always going to be appreciated for everything you do, but what you do in love is worth more than its weight in gold, and even the hardest of hearts can't fight it. Keep being you and let God deal with the rest.

#IMJUSTSAYIN...

Acts 20:35 "In everything, I showed you that by this kind of hard work we must help the weak, remembering the words of the Lord Jesus Himself: 'It is more blessed to give than to receive.'"

A PAINTED PICTURE

You just have no real motivation to do anything today. Well there's a couple of things you would love to be doing right now but because of your current situation and the way your bank account is set up... LOL (Kevin Hart). Lord knows that isn't happening no time soon. You are just totally uninterested in anything that involves you moving from that spot you're in right now. You're drained, and you just don't want to be a blessing to nobody today. As a matter of fact, what you really need is someone to be a blessing you today. Well let me tell you this, it is okay to feel that way. We all need a break sometime. We all need love, support, encouragement and all that. So, don't feel bad at all. It's all good.

NOW BREAK TIME IS OVER, GET YO BUTT UP AND DO WHAT GOD TOLD YOU. YOU DON'T GET NO BREAK WHEN IT COMES TO DOING THE WORK OF THE LORD. ON THE 7th DAY, HE RESTED. HAVE YOU DONE AS MUCH AS HE HAS IN THOSE 7 DAYS... HECK NO SO GET UP AND GET TO WORK!!!!

#IMJUSTSAYIN...

OPTIMISTIC ENERGY

Today is a new day that the Lord has made and yesterday is dead and gone. Though somethings will carry over into today don't let it consume you. Be prepared to deal with only that which you can change and accept the things that you cannot for those things are in the Lords hands.

#IMJUSTSAYIN...

Psalms 30:5
For His anger is but for a moment, His favor is for a lifetime. Weeping may endure for a night, but a shout of joy comes in the morning.

MEDITATION BREAK

No commentary just a little meditation on the word. Just read the following passages of scripture and let it minister to you. Those things that we are doing in secret will be exposed so be careful, you won't get away with it. Nothing is hidden in the eyes of God.

#IMJUSTSAYIN...

Mark 4:22 "For everything that is hidden will eventually be brought into the open, and every secret will be brought to light."
Matthew 10:26 "Fear them not therefore: for there is nothing covered, that shall not be revealed; and hid, that shall not be."
Luke 12:2 "For there is nothing covered, that shall not be revealed; neither hid, that shall not be known.
Luke 8:17 "Nothing has been covered that will not be exposed. Whatever is secret will be made known."

SEASONS CHANGE

If you are unsure of what is going on in your lives, why things don't seem to be the same, I can only associate it with the fact that some things and some people are only meant to be a part of your lives for a little while for better or worse. This helps you to experience things that you have never experienced, to grow in areas that you need work in, and to learn very valuable life lessons. Things that are needed to enrich your lives and mold you into who you are to be and to carry you into your destiny. Seasons change. They change because the world needs it, the trees, plants and vermin, animals and all living things need the elements of each season to survive. Is your season changing? Well embrace it. It's a part of life, sometimes it hurts and sometimes it doesn't. But it's needed to answer those infamous questions: Who am I? What is my purpose? Why am I here?

#IMJUSTSAYIN...

Ecclesiastes 3:3-8
3 "To everything there is a season, and a time to every purpose under the heaven:"
2 "A time to be born, and a time to die; a time to plant, and a time to pluck up that which is planted;"
3 "A time to kill, and a time to heal; a time to break down, and a time to build up;"
4 "A time to weep, and a time to laugh; a time to mourn, and a time to dance;
5 "A time to cast away stones, and a time to gather stones together; a time to embrace, and a time to refrain from embracing;"
6 "A time to get, and a time to lose; a time to keep, and a time to cast away;"
7 "A time to rend, and a time to sew; a time to keep silence, and a time to speak;"
8 "A time to love, and a time to hate; a time of war, and a time of peace."

STRAIGHT TO THE POINT

The most valuable life lesson in my mind that you need to learn, and embrace is this: One of the hardest things to do is to make your mind and body do something that the heart doesn't want to do. If your heart isn't in it then what is the point in doing it. As my Grampa used to tell us, "You are just killing time."

#IMJUSTSAYIN...

PRAYER BREAK #2

Father in the mighty name of Jesus I thank you for what you have done for me, what you are currently doing for me right now and what you plan to do in the future. My mind and heart are at peace now. Where you go I go and where I go you go!!!

#IMJUSTSAYIN...

EMBRACE THE CHANGE

I know some people are watching and don't understand what's going on in your life. What you're going through. What you're dealing with. You are a different person now, this is the new you loving life being true to yourself. You can show them better than you can tell them so don't worry about what people are saying about you. Just embrace the new you because that is what they now get. Let them get in where they fit in is all I can say cause you're doing the dang thing with or without them. I'm talking about all the naysayers, all the people that wrote you off, the ones that love to bask in your misery, the ones that you couldn't depend on for support and approval. Put God first and live life to the fullest from here on out. We all have the power to better our own lives. We don't have to sit there in depression letting others dictate our happiness. Your happiness and success reside in yourself. Stop giving everybody else the power over it and you will feel much better. Be a leader, creating a blueprint for others to follow. Let them watch how you do it in hopes that they will follow you. And if they don't well, (fill in the blank) lol...

#IMJUSTSAYIN...

OUT OF THE BLUE

You know something. It's amazing how soon people forget all the things you have done for them, all the things you've tried to do for them, and all the things you still do for them. It's so easy for people to walk all over your feelings, all over your heart like you're nothing and throw you by the wayside like a toy. All I can say is that GOD is all you need. He will never forsake you and he will never treat you like we treat each other. We will all pay for things we do to others good and bad, and even the stuff we don't know we are doing. But for real for real we know what we are doing. GOD don't like ugly y 'all. You reap what you sow just remember that as you go forward with your lives. Sow good seed so that your lives will be bountiful and wholesome.

#IMJUSTSAYIN...

THE CLOCK IS TICKING

As I sit idle, patiently waiting on what may never be, I have a lot of things on my mind. Those things brought me to this book. Writing this book has done something to me. Really pushed me into a new direction. Looking at thing's BB and AB (Before Book and After Book, LOL), I have to say, has reopened mine eyes to some things that has me dumb founded. We don't have long on this earth y 'all. We got to start living out our purpose that GOD has set for us, not the ones we have laid out for ourselves. There is no time for "let me just do this one last thing" or "I'm going to finish out the day and I will start fresh on that tomorrow." Time is of the essence. Our Lord and savior could split the clouds at any moment. Will you be in the midst of them who are called up to meet him in the air? I plan on it. I plan on being one in the midst. Figure it out people, don't get caught with your pants down around your ankles because you might not have time to pull em up. LOL.

#IMJUSTSAYIN...

FUTURISTIC PRAYER TIME

Father I asked myself this morning this specific question... "What lies ahead?" My answer was, "The unforeseen future." Today I am determined to rise above all adversity, with the supreme wisdom and knowledge of you Father to pave the way. It's the dawn of a new era. I receive it in the Mighty name of Jesus. I will now go forth and prosper...

#IMJUSTSAYIN...

HARD HEADED

My grandfather always told me, "A hard head makes a soft behind." But sometimes being hard headed is well worth it. Check it. If you're after something and you manage to get it, being hard headed isn't always a bad thing. Being hard headed can bring about change if you're being hard headed for the right reasons. Sometimes you just got to be hard headed. LOL Hard headed people tend to be more successful because they don't respond to words such and NO, THAT WONT WORK. THAT DOESN'T MAKE SENSE. THAT'S DUMB. YOU WILL NEVER FIX THAT, ETC.... In my opinion being hard headed is a form of persistence. Sometimes it can bite you in the butt, however other times like I said, it's just worth the bumps and bruises you receive. LOL. I know there's something in your life that you need to look at and just be hard headed about. I'm here to tell you that it's okay.

#IMJUSTSAYIN...

KEEP IT PUSHIN

The Devil will test you, come at you in ways you may not be prepared, but don't waiver. Keep your faith intact. Stay focused on the things he has shown you. You can't worry about what you see because the victory is in what you don't see. God is changing things as we speak and when he puts his hands on something no devil in hell can stop the process. Hold fast to what he has shown you. Keep pressing toward the mark of the high calling. And always remember that Rome was not built in a day.

#IMJUSTSAYIN...

BREAKING THE CHAINS

My God, My God Is Breaking Chains. Press thru because he's going to knock all THE WALLS down. It has begun. Watch, your life is going to change right before your eyes, if you believe in what he has shown you, and where he is taking you. The journey will be tough, but it won't be long. Many people are going to fall away, just don't fret, stay steadfast and let him work. Keep your mind and your heart pure. Prayer is the best tool for you in this time.

#IMJUSTSAYIN...

James 5:16 "Confess your faults one to another, and pray one for another, that ye may be healed. The effectual fervent prayer of a righteous man availeth much."

FINANCIAL PROSPERITY

Inspired by a book I read called, "Power Over All Devils and Evil " Here's an Excerpt from the text. Let it resonate in your spirit.

Financial Prosperity comes from God. In Fact, no matter what you do, if God has made up His mind that you will never prosper financially, you cannot prosper financially. If you like, go to the strongest secret society or witch-doctor, if God says you will die today, you cannot see tomorrow. Even, all the things Satan boasts of cannot be if God says, "Enough is enough." He who trusts in the devil or in man is a fool. He who says that the Lord does not see has no understanding. Financial prosperity is a product of obedience, faith, hard work, giving, and diligence. You cannot maintain these five virtues permanently and not prosper financially. Faith will bring what does not exist to existence. Obedience will make you follow God's plan for your life and to obey His Word. Hard work will make you invest your resources and energy to the cause you are pursuing; Giving will bring multiplication and increase to your seed and offerings; and diligence will produce consistency. Physical prosperity is a function of Divine Intervention and obedience to physical laws. God's word is medicine to your body. He sends forth His word, and His word heals the sick.

#IMJUSTSAYIN...

ARE YOU ON A ONEWAY?

Your life is not your own. To Him you belong so give in and give yourself to him.

Hey, this is for all you lovers out there... Love is a two-way street and relationships are two-way streets. Taking care of each other is a two-way street. Making each other feel loved is a two-way street. If you look at your situation and it appears that you have been on a one-way street for a long time? Then maybe you should think about turning the corner. Left hand turns are legal on a one-way even at a stoplight. You can always make a right turn as well, but if you can't figure it out, just make a dang U-turn and head the other way.... LOL...

#IMJUSTSAYIN...

BACK STORY

My inspiration comes from my own trials and triumphs. I post my experiences on social media in hopes that it will reach people who may be going thru something similar. That is also the reason I have written this book. If you really read this book with an open mind and a pure heart, and not just trying to figure out what's going on with me and let the words minister to you. You just might find a blessing in the words.

One of the hardest things to do is to let go and let GOD. But, I'm telling you, when you do, Man! Doors start to open, those needs he dang sure starts to supply. Your destiny starts to manifest itself. Continue to be diligent in your walk, following his guidance and watch your life flourish in this foreign place called earth. For we are in this world but we are not of this world. There is a better place being prepared for us. But until then, live your life in a manner pleasing to God and enjoy it to the fullest.

#IMJUSTSAYIN...

SHORT AND SWEET

Sometimes you got to do life just the way it is dealt to you. Play it out. Do not fold.

IT JUST MIGHT TURN OUT TO BE THE WINNING HAND...

#IMJUSTSAYIN...

DON'T LET HURT & PAIN HARDEN YOUR HEART

You know something y'all, the devil sure does try to do everything in his power to change you, to turn you into something that you are not. Using every tactic in his arsenal to make you react in a negative manner. Don't ever give him the power. Remain true to who you are. Do not become an unloving, uncaring person just because of past hurts and pains. The things you have done, the support you have given, the love you have provided, whether noticed or unnoticed remains even if the portrait is being painted in a different light. Christ walked this earth doing nothing but good things, but they still tried to paint a negative picture of him to justify his crucifixion. What they didn't understand is why it never affected him or his purpose here on earth. They didn't realize that what they were doing was fulfilling his destiny, which was to die for our sins, the redemption of the world. He never changed who he was, he never gave in to the nonsense rising around him even though he could have he never retaliated. He just continued to love and forgive.

Luke 23:34 "Father forgive them for they know not what they do."

All I'm saying is past loves, relationships, friendships, marriages, jobs, failed businesses, backbiting, vengeful people, HATERS, etc., are just the tools being used to mold you into who you are or who you are to be. Press through because in the end God's love will prevail, God's protection of you will never forsake you at any cost. KILL THAT CRAZINESS WITH LOVE AND KINDNESS. Love anyway, be kind, be the better person, endure persecution.

Proverbs 19:11 "A man's discretion makes him slow to anger, and it is his glory to overlook a transgression."

#IMJUSTSAYIN...

CRAZY YOUNG FOLK

You young folks are doing WAY too much these days. Do you all even really think things through thoroughly before you all decide to do something? Cause it sure don't seem like it. So, if you're reading this book, I'm going to help you out. Before you decide to do something that could very well change the course of the rest of your life, especially in a negative manner, ask yourself these three simple questions. This is something my football players and the young people that I mentor know all too well.

1. Will this get me in trouble?
2. Can I end up in jail?
3. Will this affect my life negatively in anyway?

If The answer is even maybe to either of them then the odds are 100 times out of a 100 that you shouldn't do it...

#IMJUSTSAYIN...

A STRONG OPINIONATED MESSAGE TO THE LADIES.

This will be a hard pill to swallow for some of you. You know something Ladies, and I'm not talking to all of you but for real, I'm sick and tired of all this male bashing, sexist BS you all be posting and plastering all over the internet and different places. We are not all bad come on now. The lot of us are descent very hard-working dudes. Some more than others, some a bit down on their luck but striving to do what they can to survive. The crap some of us must put up with just to make some of you all happy is just unreal. You all talk about us like we are sheep poo poo on a muddy road as my grandfather used to say. LOL. All because your gold-digging self-centered behinds can't appreciate what a hardworking man is out there already doing, trying to provide for you and yours. But hey that's not good enough cause you want more. EVERY SUCCESSFUL MAN DIDN'T HAVE A STRONG WOMAN BEHIND THEM. They had a nut ball that wouldn't buy into his vision or dream to help him. He had to go at it alone while you made him feel unworthy and inadequate. We all are not OBAMA and the lot of you all are not no DANG MICHELLE either. It's not our fault you got a rotten apple. Shoot, times are hard and neither you nor we have time for that mess. That's why some of you are all by yourself and you will never find that soul mate. He might be staring you right in the face and you don't see him because he drives a bucket and don't have a house in the hills. But he is working two jobs trying to support his own business but because it may not have taken off yet, he's nothing in your eyes. You can't even see his worth. LET ME TELL SOME OF YOU SOMETHING. SOME OF YOU AIN'T CRAP EITHER OR YOUR MINDSET WOULD BE DIFFERENT. We been through some crap with some of Y 'all too, you guys are not innocent either. Some out there posting they bodies and twerking and all that mess, CHEATING ON YOUR HUSBANDS AND BOYFRIENDS AND WHAT NOT JUST LIKE MEN. And trying to justify it by saying men been doing it for years. Well if we jumped off a building and went splat, would you do that to? Might as well. And trying to play the role like you don't do nothing when you are no better than the men you are bashing. And then you wonder why you attract so many bad men in your life. HAVE SOME RESPECT FOR YOUR DANG SELF AND MAYBE YOU WILL FIND THE RIGHT GUY...

NO MAN WANTS A FACEBOOK HOE... YEAH, I SAID IT... DONT NO MAN WANT A WOMAN THAT EVERYBODY HAS ACCESS TO...

Now here's the key... If you got mad at what you just read, then you are guilty, and I am talking to you. But if you understood what I said then you understand that every woman isn't included in this rant. My point to you all is this. Stop grouping all men in your hurt and pain because you might miss out on the one who has been sent to help you heal.

#IMJUSTSAYIN...

MORE ENCOURAGEMENT

There is always going to be somethings that will try to impede your destiny, success and pursuit for happiness, but hold fast to your faith and stay on the path. Don't worry about who is on board and who is not. Just keep it pushing and press toward the mark of the high calling and GOD will make all things new. You will achieve a greater reward in the end.

#IMJUSTSAYIN...

STOP LOOKING BACKWARD

IF YOU KEEP WASTING TIME LOOKING BACKWARD ON WHAT YOU COULD HAVE DONE AND SHOULD HAVE DONE TO MAKE YOUR LIFE BETTER YOU WILL LOSE FOCUS ON WHAT YOU ARE ABOUT TO BECOME AND WHERE YOUR LIFE IS ABOUT TO GO. WHATS DONE IS DONE. TIME TO MOVE FORWARD. MAKE NEW MEMORIES, EXPERIENCE NEW THINGS AND EMBRACE YOUR NEW FUTURE. WHATS DONE IS DONE AND WHAT WILL BE IS YET TO COME!!!

#IMJUSTSAYIN...

GOD SPEED THE SPEED OF LIFE

When GOD starts to move in your life some things tend to seem unreal. Things start to happen so fast that you think that it is too good to be true. You then start to second guess yourself and start to try to slow things down, but all you are doing is impeding GOD's plan for your life. Not to mention, the Devil is just trying to prevent you from reaching your destiny. If you feel these things starting to happen, pray and keep moving forward. When GOD moves, he moves just like that, and he moves swiftly. Roll with it, and you just might get to where he is taking you. We pray for his blessings, we pray for his favor in our lives, on our jobs, in our businesses, in our marriages, etc., then when he moves we get nervous, scared, worried. We start listening to other people who aren't GOD and all they do is start putting more worry into your spirit. "Are you sure you're ready for that?" "I would wait a little longer." "Why are you moving so fast?" "Take your time!" Hey, some of it is hate, some is genuine concern but nonetheless it can be just enough discouragement to satisfy the devil's plan to stop you from walking into GOD's glory. Three things I leave you with:

1. IGNORE... It's the devil.
2. PRAY.... Remove the negativity.
3. PERSEVERE... Walk into your blessing.

#IMJUSTSAYIN

BOO THANGS

There are Boo Thangs all around us. For those of you that don't have a Boo Thang or that keep hooking up with the wrong Boo Thang. My advice to you is to sit back and listen to God. Then open your eyes and you will see that he put your Boo Thang right where you can grab 'em. But haste not because your Boo Thang might disappear if you wait too long to grab 'em up, because one person's trash is another person's Boo Thang!!!!

#BOOTHANGS
#IMJUSTSAYIN...

THE PAST IS THE PAST

Hey y 'all, it's that great inspirational Kat you all know as Zimm here 'bout to hit you with some more insights straight from the dome.

THE PAST, IS EXACTLY WHAT IT IS, THE PAST. LET IT GO. You can't fix it, you can't change it, no matter how hard you try it is what it is, and you must move on with your life. I'm sure if we all had the opportunity to go back into time and redo some things the lot of us would jump at that opportunity. But guess what? Not going to happen. So, what are you going to do about it? My point is this, and not to contradict my opening statement. You can't change the past but you can fix it. And that's by creating a new past. But the only way is to build a bright new future....

#IMJUSTSAYIN...

HOW MANY TIMES DO YOU REALLY FALL IN LOVE?

There are some things that you will never be exposed to but find yourself caught up in it because of your struggles. I found this somewhere on the internet a long time ago, not sure if the site is even up anymore but, I FIND IT TO BE %100 TRUE AT LEAST FOR ME. AND THANKS TO MY MOST HIGH GOD I BELIEVE I HAVE ARRIVED. MAY THESE FEW WORDS BLESS YOU AS YOU READ IT.

It is a common belief that each person falls in love three times during their lifetime. However, each one of these happen under a very different light from the one before and each serves a very different purpose.

THE FIRST LOVE
The first love happens when we are young, sometimes as young as the time we are in high school. This love fulfills the dreams of our youth and fulfills our idealistic belief of what we expect love to look like – just like the fairy tales. This love fulfills our need to live up to society's expectations. We jump into this love headfirst believing that this person will be our only love (even if it does not feel quite right) and convince ourselves that this is how love should look. This love focuses more on how others perceive us versus how we feel.

THE SECOND LOVE
The next love, the second love, is the hard love. This is the love that teaches us lessons about ourselves and how we need to feel love in any relationship. This love brings with it great pain – the pain of loss, deceit and lies.

During this love we believe we are doing things differently, but we are not. We tend to hold steadfast to this love because this relationship is different from the last one. However, this one is the one where we will grow.

This is the one where we will experience pain. And this is the love where we will realize what we really need out of our next relationship. The issue with this love is it can tend to become cyclical – repeating the same issues over and over and expecting a different result. Unfortunately, each time through the cycle the ending is worse.

This love is often unhealthy and rather unbalanced. During this love there can be emotional or physical abuse and often there is some form of manipulation at play. This love is surrounded by a constant state of drama and this drama is the reason we hold on. The drama becomes addictive and it becomes hard to break the cycle. This love brings with it a strong need to make things work versus focusing on if the relationship is working. This is the love we hoped would last forever.

THE THIRD
The last love is the love that comes out of left field. This is the love that surprises us and destroys any ideas of what we believed our love should look like. This love is easy, and we wonder how it is possible that love could be this simple and has no complications. It is the love that sweeps us off our feet because we were not looking for a relationship. This is the love where everything feels as though it is falling perfectly into place. This love is uncomplicated and is not filled with expectations. Perfection is not something we feel pressure to achieve and find ourselves perfectly content in our lives and our relationship.

This love does not look like the love we dreamed we would have, and this love does not follow any of the rules we had set up for ourselves. This love breaks any notions we had about what our greatest love would look like and shatters any beliefs of how we thought it would be. This love just simply feels right. It is the love that has been knocking at our doors for ages and we finally decided to answer. It is the love that teaches us how to feel love and to give love.

You may not have experienced all three of these loves yet, but perhaps it is because you are just not ready for each love. Love is an experience – it deserves processing and appreciation. You might find that you only have one love during your lifetime. Do not fret, you are not required to have multiples loves during your lifetime. Your journey to that third love is not identical to any other person's journey. Your journey is yours only and you will be the only one to experience your love story.

No matter where you are in the cycle of love – the ideal love, the broken love or the perfect love – you will find that you can learn something in each love. Because each love provides us the ability to find that perfect love. The love that lasts. The love that proves that your other loves were not supposed to work.

#IMJUSTSAYIN...

WHEN GOD MOVES YOU MOVE

When GOD moves, you move, Just like that. When HE moves, you move, JUST LIKE THAT!!!

When God starts to move in your life, we tend to start asking a whole lot of questions instead of just rolling with it. What's the use in praying if we're just going to 20 question the way he answers, then we end up losing out on a much-needed breakthrough in our lives. Don't question GOD. JUST DO IT!!! Because YOU DESERVE A BREAK TODAY!!! Just remember you can't always HAVE IT YOUR WAY!!! So, when you're done questioning his answers and messing up things, turn it over and leave it to him. It's not too late, it's just delayed and trust me, HE WILL LEAVE THE LIGHT ON FOR YOU!!! So, I say again...

When GOD moves, you move, just like that. When HE moves, you move, just like that. When GOD moves you move, just like that.... Hey DJ, wait a minute. Bring that back... When HE moves, you move, just like that. When GOD moves, you move, just like that. When HE moves, you move. When GOD moves, you move, JUST LIKE THAT!!! Thanks Ludacris for helping me get my point across.

#IMJUSTSAYIN...

BE THANKFUL

Today's going to be a good day do you know why? Because you're going to be thankful for the little things that the Lord does for you every day, and just when you think that you don't have the things you need to make it through today, if you stay cool, calm and collected and you just marinate on the fact that he said that he will supply all your needs. You will find that everything that you need to make it through this day is sitting right there in front of you. So just go slam-dunk your day. ARE YOU WITH ME?

#IMJUSTSAYIN...

BOO THANGS PART II

A good Boo Thang will make you feel like you can conquer the world.
A good Boo Thang will make you feel like the president.
A good Boo Thang will make you feel like me. Lol.
If you don't have A good Boo Thang yet, man u missing out.
And if the Boo Thang you do have don't make you feel like that.
Then maybe you have the wrong Boo Thang.
And you just might need to trade that Boo Thang in.

#IMJUSTSAYIN...

LEAVE YOUR EGO AT THE DOOR

So, check this out as I've been sitting here writing and thinking about ministry, my place in ministry, what God called me to do and how he called me to do it. Why he called me to do it. I started thinking about it a lot more because you know when God gives you a word, it self-checks you first. So, what he has told me to do is to promote life and love and true happiness. Showing the world growth even through the midst of a storm, being totally transparent even throughout my own struggles with life, which brings me to my message for this segment.

For a while I've been hearing a few preachers talk about Internet preachers and all that stuff. And I know God in his word compelled us to go out and spread his word, spread the gospel across the world using whatever tools that we have in front of us to do so. And last time I checked, social media especially in this day and age is one of those tools that we surely should be using to help get the word out there, seeing how that's where most of the people are. But that's not really my issue. My issue is the people that come down on those of us who choose to use social media for that purpose. So, here's where my issue lies. And this to me is a double standard. If I post a message, a sermon or something spiritually uplifting that would help out a person or cause someone to turn to Christ or make a change or whatever. Or pray for someone online out in the open or what have you, directly on Facebook, Instagram etc. And you preach across a pulpit and post your sermon, church video, stream your service online or whatever. ISN'T THAT THE SAME THING? Is it different because you do it from inside of the church and I don't? What makes what you do different from what I do especially if we both have a license and we both are called to Preach? Don't we just choose different tools and platforms to do it? What makes what I do wrong and what you do right? Maybe it's because I don't follow the traditional ways of the church that we have all been programmed to believe is the only way God can reach people. And I'm not confused, because I know what God meant when he said forsake not the assembly of ourselves.

Are we not all doing God's work? What makes those of us that use social media wrong? This just something to make you think. Just know this if you post your sermon online you are no different than me. Leave your ego at the door...

#IMJUSTSAYIN...

JOY WILL COME IN THE MORNING

When you can't seem to find those that were supposed to stand with you and you find yourself standing alone, do not be discouraged, keep pressing through, keep being diligent and follow through with the process. Those others that have fallen by the wayside will return to you with their hand out upon your success. They just don't believe in the vision that you have and all they would do is pull against it anyway, so it's best that you go at it alone. Don't waver, stand firm, stand strong, you're at the brink of your breakthrough, and all you need is you and the Lord above to break the chains. No negative energy allowed on your journey. Satan will try to destroy your vision and faith, but remember it is always darkest before the dawn. Beyond every dark cloud is a silver lining and after each rainstorm there's a brand-new joy. When trouble grieves you and all your friends deceive you, don't you worry because it will pass over in the morning. Weeping may endure for a night but joy cometh in the morning!!!

#IMJUSTSAYIN...

RANDOM THOUGHT

The holidays are upon us. Do you know your worth? You know it's not all about the gifts, right? Do you know your Savior? Find your happy place. Be cheerful and merry givers for it is better to give than it is to receive. Tell everyone you know that are close to you that you love them. Take nothing for granted because it may not be there tomorrow. Well heck, you might not be there tomorrow.

#IMJUSTSAYIN...

JUST BE YOURSELF

You know as I sit here meditating, writing and praying, I have come to the realization that no matter what you do, no matter how well you write things or say things, no matter how good you mean for things to be or how positive you are in life, no matter how much positivity you try to promote, no matter how much good you try to do, there is always going to be someone that takes offense to what you do or to what you say. But, I say to all who takes the time to read this, all you really can do is take everything with a grain of salt turn it all over to God himself and let him sort out the rest. Misunderstandings and oversights being taken as purposely initiated actions however simple minded it may be does happen on a very regular basis. All we can do as a people is strive to be better people, to understand one another, to help one another, to uplift one another. There are definitely times when we all get overlooked, what does that mean? Does it mean we're not loved or appreciated? No, it doesn't. It just means we were overlooked that particular time. Now we can talk about each other with other people and create issues or we can talk to each other to resolve issues, it's a choice we make as a people. But because of social media people have gotten to be so impersonal, and to the point that we don't even pick up the phone anymore. Shame on us. We knit pick at things people post just to find fault in it. However, it is the way of the world. Life's too short to have nonsense build between family, friends, coworkers, church members and so on and so forth. The Bible says if you have an ought against your brother go to them. Why let things fester and build until it creates pain and anguish inside. All that does is cause us to generate gossiping and backbiting, all of that nonsense when all you have to do is talk. I will never understand why people don't understand that it's that simple. I do pray that one day we all get it together because the world would surely be a better place to live in.

#IMJUSTSAYIN...

FAILURE IS A TOOL FOR SUCCESS

People that are scared to fail will never achieve their maximum potential. The reason is because they are too scared to take a chance, scared because they may run out of money, scared because they may lose a job, scared because they may lose a friend, scared because it's out of their comfort zone. How can you learn if you don't make a mistake? You can plan your life to the T and live structured and safe if that is what makes you happy, but are you satisfied with just a few thousand dollars extra in the bank. Those that strive to be millionaires and entrepreneurs, how are you going to make that first million dollars if you are too scared to take chances. How are you going to find that true love if you are scared to get back in the game due to past hurts.

STOP BEING SCARED AND TAKE SOME CHANCES. THE WORST YOU CAN DO IS FAIL!!! BUT IF AT FIRST YOU DON'T SUCCEED!!!! TRY IT AGAIN BUT LEARN FROM THE LAST EXPERIENCE AND CHANGE THE GAME PLAN AND MAKE IT HAPPEN!!! DON'T JUST GIVE UP!!!

#IMJUSTSAYIN...

SEPARATE YOURSELF

Sometimes life brings things around that makes you think, things that force you to make tough decisions, things that pull on your energy source in a negative or positive way, and you have to figure out a way to deal with those things and make them work for you. Sometimes the best way to do that is to separate yourself from the negative to prevent yourself from being tempted to engage in those things that drain on your energy source. That way you can focus on what's really important. So, you can engage the positive things in your life. Then your mind will be open and more receptive to the things that are most important. So, don't sit there and allow those things that pull on your energy source take up all of your time and attention because it takes away from the time and attention that can be spent on the things that they should be spent on, like goals and dreams. Be smart about your life choices. Be smart about your words in secret and aloud. Be smart about that inner voice that we all have and take time to reflect before you speak, looking at the consequences of all things good and bad. At the end of the day just do your best to make smarter choices in life. Trust me it goes along way!!!

E + R = O, The EVENT is going to happen, and it is something that you have no control over, your RESPONSE to that event you do have control over, and that's what controls the OUTCOME!!!

#IMJUSTSAYIN...

UP UP UP YOUR DIRECTION IS UP

IF YOU FEEL LIKE YOU HAVE HIT ROCK BOTTOM AND LIFE AS YOU KNEW IT IS OVER, FRET NOT, YOU'RE IN THE GREATEST PLACE YOU CAN BE!!! TAKE IT FROM ME. THE ONLY PLACE LEFT TO GO IS UP!!!

#IMJUSTSAYIN...

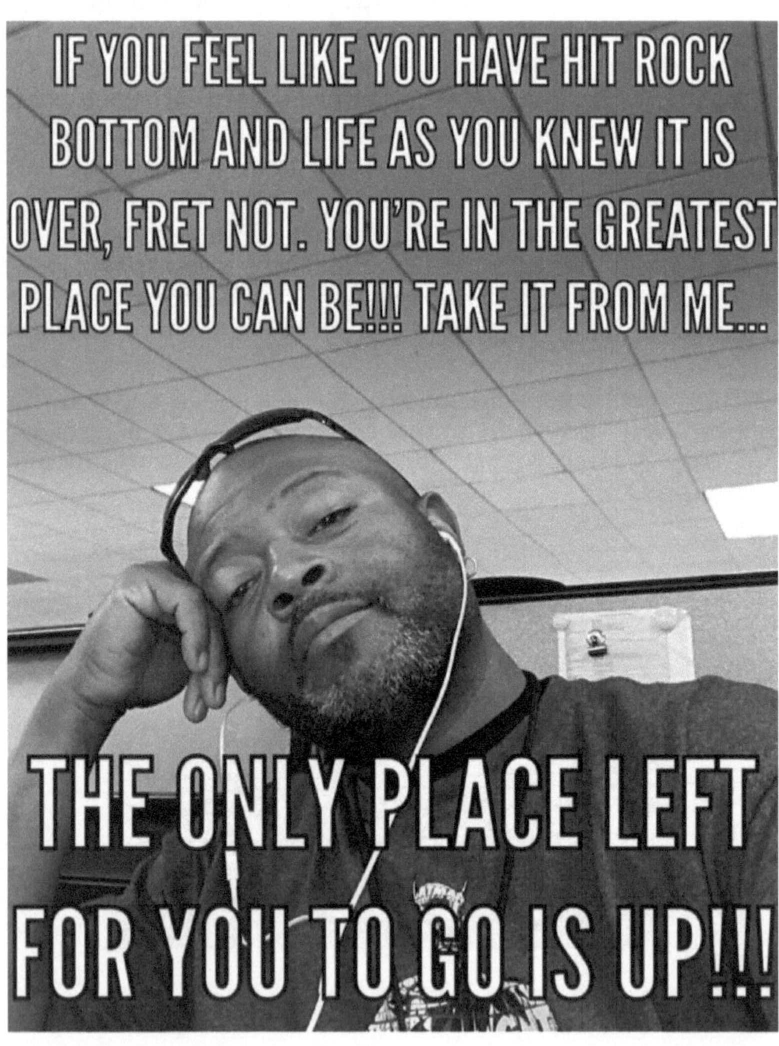

67

JUST SAYIN'

69

INDEX

INDEX

ABOUT THE AUTHOR

Elder Zimmeri C. McNeal Jr. isn't a house hold name. However, this book will definitely make his readers remember him. He has an extensive religious, musical and technical background that advances his artistry and craftsmanship. He is well versed in all aspects of Ministry, Audio/Video recording from both pre and post-production aspects, to include music production, audio sweetening, filming, lighting, audio/video editing, writing, recording, mixing, and mastering etc. He is a fast paced, fast learning upbeat type of guy who has tunnel vision towards success. His goal setting seems somewhat unrealistic to others but his strong faith in God makes him that way as he works vigorously to achieve them. He has a street like outlook on life and a strong keep it real attitude toward everything he does and says. That's why you are going to love this book, the first of many to come. He lives in Aurora, Colorado with his wife Kimyetta and his dog Snoopy where he owns and operates his commercial recording studio (Zimtek Studios).